Tales of the
# Celebrity Hermit

St Robert 800

# Tales of the
# Celebrity Hermit

**by Peter Lacey**

The encounters of
St Robert of Knaresborough
An historical fiction

Written to commemorate
the 800th anniversary
of the death of St Robert

Published by Peter Lacey
2018

Text copyright © 2018 Peter Lacey

Cover images © Shutterstock.com Monk Figure Praying in the Forest by Rudy Bagozzi, Watercolour Silhouettes of Men and Women by Cat_arch_angel

King John image © Adobe Stock Georgios Kollidas

St Robert illustrations © Shirley Vine

All rights reserved. This book or any portion thereof may not be reproduced or used in any manner whatsoever without the express written permission of the publisher except for the use of brief quotations in a book review or scholarly journal.

First Printing: 2018

ISBN: 978-0-244-36452-6

www.strobertofknaresborough.org.uk/

All profits from the sale of this book will go to supporting events associated with the 800$^{th}$ anniversary and building a legacy for St Robert in Knaresborough.

# Dedication

*For my brother Rob, who knew the power of story and lived his life to tell the best story of all time.*

# Contents

Acknowledgements ................................................................ x
Historical note and comment on sources ........................... xi
Preface ..................................................................................... xii
Navigating your way through St Robert's life ...................... xiv
Timeline .................................................................................. xv

## Stories:

A Mother's Regret .................................................................... 1
Lost and Found ...................................................................... 19
A Broken Bow ........................................................................ 31
Flashes of Hope ..................................................................... 43
A Clash of Kingdoms ............................................................. 59
A Band of Brothers ................................................................ 73

# Acknowledgements

I would like to thank Daniel Ingram-Brown for his encouragement and coaching in my journey to become a story-teller; Heather Wheeler for her initial proofing of the text; to many others who have added their own inspiration to the stories in this book; and to my wife, Gilly, who put up with my regular musings and occasional pre-occupation with all things St Robert!

# Historical note and comment on sources

I have departed knowingly from the accepted story of St Robert only once, which is in choosing the name Helena de Plompton for St Robert's main benefactor, rather than Juliana. Having reviewed available genealogies and sought to match them to the emerging timeline of St Robert's life and the personal circumstances of this benefactor, I have found that Helena de Plompton is a better fit. I trust that others will understand this small departure, which takes nothing from the overall impact of her role in helping to establish Robert in his ministry.

My main inspiration for these stories has been Dr Frank Bottomley's translation of the Latin biography written in c.1250 by a Trinitarian friar at the priory which succeeded Robert's hermitage. Other sources have included online genealogies and articles that bring the period in which St Robert lived to life. For these and other materials, as well as the activities associated with his 800th anniversary in the market town of Knaresborough, in the beautiful county of North Yorkshire, please visit:

**www.strobertofknaresborough.org.uk**

# Preface

Robert Flower (c.1160-1218), or St Robert of Knaresborough as we have come to know him, lived 800 years ago. He was brought up in a well-to-do family in a prosperous and growing region of a Europe that was still taking shape after the Norman conquest of the British Isles. Robert's home town of York, and his adopted community in Knaresborough, provide the immediate setting for our stories, but the influences and reflections from a larger canvass are never far away.

Whilst we describe St Robert as a 'hermit', such a title belies the interaction he had with the world around him – one academic looking into his legacy has described him as 'the celebrity hermit of Knaresborough'[1]. As a boy growing up in a family that was 'numbered in the upper classes' his education would have been well rounded, and the conversations he would have been part of at home, and in the streets, markets and taverns, would have ranged widely. We can only imagine, for example, what he might have made of the recent murder of Thomas a Becket in Canterbury Cathedral, and the fact that the murderous knights had fled to the nearby castle at Knaresborough for safety.

There is no doubt that when established in St Robert's Cave, sometime in the 1190's, he was becoming

---

[1] Hazel Blair, "St Robert: the celebrity hermit of Knaresborough", *Region and Nation in Late Medieval Devotion to Northern English Saints* (blog), 25 August 2017, https://wp.unil.ch/regionandnation/2017/08/the-celebrity-hermit-of-knaresborough/

something of a celebrity. He was visited and spoken about across Europe, and he would have had the opportunity to find out about many of the events in the world around him. His regular engagement with visitors from far and wide, as well as with the 'people of the tower', which is something he might have called his beloved Knaresborians, pricked his conscience and on many occasions prompted him to action.

He might, for example, have known about the cost of King Richard's ransom in 1193, which was required to secure his return from the crusades. Taking account of inflation, this has been estimated by some historians as costing somewhere in the region of two and a half to three billion pounds in today's money. Robert would have understood something of how that would impact on the levels of taxation for the poor – he was, of course, a contemporary of Robin Hood. Perhaps also, the way that he responded to King John when he visited the cave hinted strongly that Robert was aware of the conflicts between the Crown and the English Barons, as well as between the Crown and the Church in Rome.

But the stories told in this book are also very personal. They reflect on a journey that one man took to discover his purpose in a world that presented exciting opportunities, and yet often left a mess from failures to live properly in community. There are echoes of Grenfell Tower, of thuggery and hardship, and of over-officious bureaucracies; but also, of warm family gatherings, devotion to service and of hope.

# Navigating your way through St Robert's life

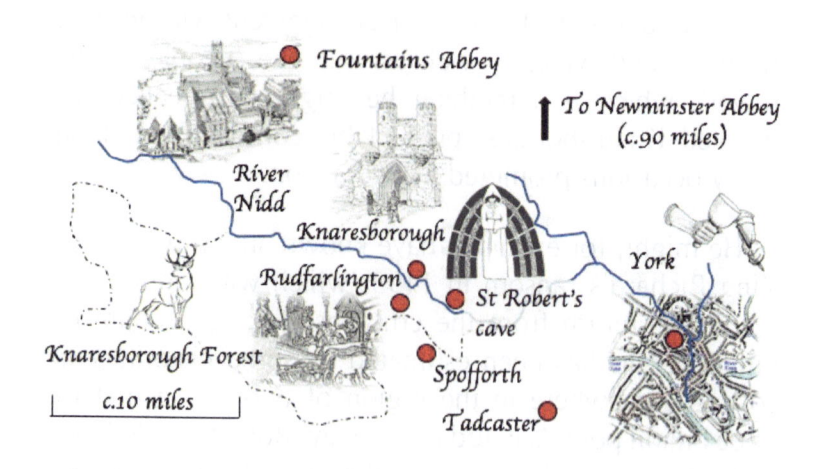

## Some of the people in St Robert's circle:

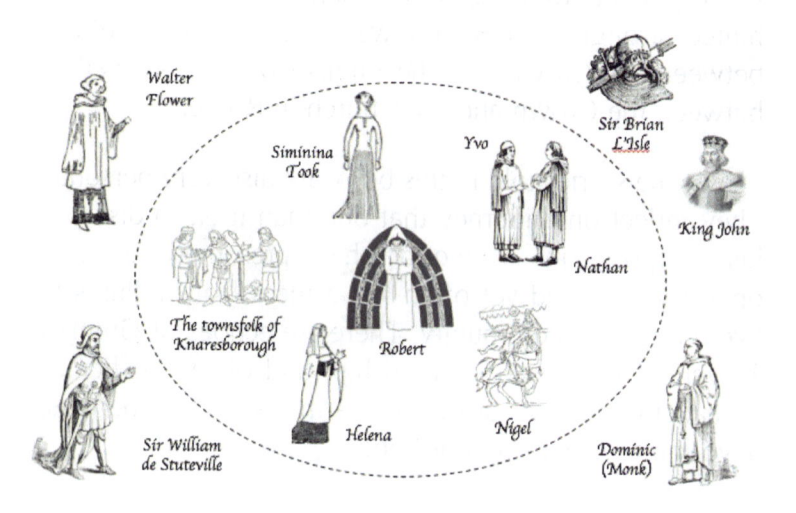

- Walter Flower
- Siminina Took
- Yvo
- Sir Brian L'Isle
- King John
- The townsfolk of Knaresborough
- Robert
- Nathan
- Helena
- Nigel
- Dominic (Monk)
- Sir William de Stuteville

# Timeline

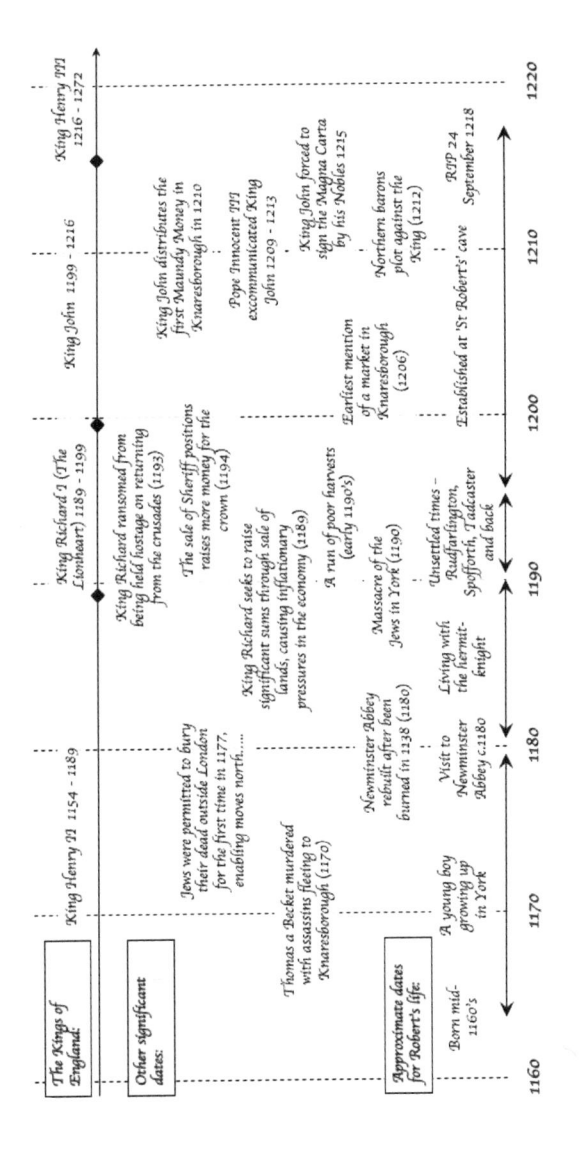

**The Kings of England:**
- King Henry II 1154 - 1189
- King Richard I (The Lionheart) 1189 - 1199
- King John 1199 - 1216
- King Henry III 1216 - 1272

**Other significant dates:**
- Thomas a Becket murdered with assassins fleeing to Knaresborough (1170)
- Jews were permitted to bury their dead outside London for the first time in 1177, enabling moves north....
- Newminster Abbey rebuilt after been burned in 1138 (1180)
- King Richard ransomed from being held hostage on returning from the crusades (1193)
- King Richard seeks to raise significant sums through sale of lands, causing inflationary pressures in the economy (1189)
- The sale of Sheriff positions raises more money for the crown (1194)
- Massacre of the Jews in York (1190)
- A run of poor harvests (early 1190's)
- Earliest mention of a market in Knaresborough (1206)
- King John distributes the first Maundy Money in Knaresborough in 1210
- Pope Innocent III excommunicated King John 1209 - 1213
- King John forced to sign the Magna Carta by his Nobles 1215
- Northern barons plot against the King (1212)

**Approximate dates for Robert's life:**
- Born mid-1160's
- A young boy growing up in York
- Visit to Newminster Abbey c.1180
- Living with the hermit-knight
- Unsettled times – Rudfarlington, Spofforth, Tadcaster and back
- Established at St Robert's cave
- RIP 24 September 1218

1160 — 1170 — 1180 — 1190 — 1200 — 1210 — 1220

xv

# A Mother's Regret

Siminina (St Robert's mother)   Walter Flower (and his brother)

### Sometime around the mid 1180's & then later in mid-late 1190's

Mother's passing left a hole at the centre of our family. In our happier memories that gap had been filled by the fun loving, ever ambitious, mother and wife, in a home that thrived on visitors, particularly when there was some wine to sample — mother's line of business you understand.

When I, and my older brother Robert, used to play in the yard, there was always the watchful eye of mother.

Ambitious for us both, and happy to see us take the little risks that boys take — getting in and out of scrapes together, we knew that she was always there if needed.

But in her last few months, following the court case, mother had become something of a recluse, a hermit in her own home, unable to show her face to the outside world. She did not die happy, though our memories are of better times.

My father and I were returning from the funeral. It was an early winter's day with the frost just melting and a bright sun, low in the sky, catching us on occasion as we wound our way back through the narrow streets of York to the house. As we opened the door we paused briefly. With the cold on our backs, and the emptiness of the house in front, we looked to the right where the kitchen had once been filled with mother's presence as she provided for her family, and then to the left where a storeroom had been the hub of her wine selling business.

It was in the storeroom, now empty apart from a single chair, an upturned wine barrel and some dusty shelves, that mother had spent her last weeks. Sitting, staring, thinking, occasionally writing. Little conversation had passed during that time, though both myself and father often sat with her, ready to listen.

As we stood staring into the house the sun shone through the window into the storeroom in a way that was only possible on a small number of days each year. It cast a dark shadow where the sun didn't reach, but a vibrant dance of dust particles and spider webs where it shone its light. The room seemed to draw me in, and I wondered whether an impulse to sit in mother's chair for a few moments was morbid, or an expression of love for the person who gave us so much. I sat.

Perhaps because I'd never seen the room from this angle, or simply because of the sun shining through the window, I noticed little things that I'd not seen before. It was as if the precise positioning of the chair and the upturned barrel retained something of the feelings that mother had struggled to express in those final weeks.

In the stark emptiness of the room I saw the dents in the floor where the barrels had landed over the years in a repeated fashion. I saw stains on the handles of the drawers in which documents had been kept. I saw a series of notches or nicks in the window frame, those at the bottom looking old and smooth but becoming increasingly fresh and sharp edged as you cast your eyes up the frame.

And then I noticed a parchment tucked into the side of the wine barrel, as if hanging there ready for the next entry in a ledger or stock book. I reached out, took it from the side of the barrel, and opened it. In mother's clear hand I read the following...

*To my dearest Robert*

*I don't know if this letter will get to you, but I feel so troubled that unless I write it all down I might drown. It's been difficult to write, partly because I've lost all the drive that used to make life so full.*

# PETER LACEY

*I remember the things we shared when you were growing up. Going to the market was always a highlight. You used to ask where all the food came from, and why some people seemed to have so much to sell when others didn't. And then there were the discussions we had when you returned from visiting Holy Trinity, or from marveling at the Minster, which seemed to be in constant development. You were always able to fathom out when things seemed right, or wrong, even if we couldn't fathom exactly why — oh how I have needed that since you left us.*

*I'm sat in the storeroom staring at the wooden beam across the window looking out to the yard. Everything is quiet now. No sounds of the cart wheels and the whinnying horses looking for refreshment after hauling their goods into our storehouse. All that's left is a single empty wine barrel standing on its end to make the simple table on which I'm leaning to write.*

*On the wooden beam are marks, chinks in the sturdy oak that I made on each anniversary of you leaving. Twenty chinks in the wood. Nobody else notices them, but each one is pregnant with missed opportunities. But perhaps you've found a new way to be, a different way, a way that sorts out the crazy world around us that's so full of plans and joy one day, but then turns around and kicks you in the teeth. How different might things have been, Robert, if you'd stayed and been part of our family. I don't blame you, but there's been a hole in my life.*

*I don't know if you've picked up the news about what's happened here recently. I'm deeply ashamed and angry about it. We've lost some really precious friends and now, to add insult to injury, I've been hauled before the magistrates.*

*I need to tell you the story...*

*You'll remember Jacob and Elizabeth, and their son Nathan who you used to play with. And you'll no doubt remember the conversations we had about their Jewish faith, something that was clearly a sensitive subject, what with the crusades going on, but honestly these were God-fearing people who just wanted to play their part in society.*

*What you don't know is that because they had maintained good links with people across the channel they made ideal trading partners for my little wine business. And this became even more important soon after you left us when it became illegal for us Christians to charge interest on loans. I'd come to rely on small amounts of money from a number of people because of the time it took for our wine to reach the customer, and our customers wouldn't pay up front for fear of 'loss in transit', something not so unusual when the roads are so dangerous. So, Jacob and Elizabeth became an integral part of funding our business, and small payments of interest to reflect their investment was, in my view, entirely appropriate, and legal.*

*But things got out of hand when people found themselves relying more and more on this type of money lending. Instead of using loans to fund a going concern, many had to rely on them for filling gaps that just seemed to grow. It was nobody's doing, but circumstances started* to combine in an ominous way. Storm clouds were gathering, and we were completely helpless in the face of the gradual gloom creeping over the business world. I felt hemmed in when making decisions, surviving by the skin of my teeth, but stories about business failure that used to be rare began to be the subject of conversation on a regular basis.

First there was the way that money was being drained from the system by the Crown. Many of the local landowners had been 'encouraged' to buy land from the King to fuel the war effort. It wasn't exactly a tax, but not to comply would have been viewed as very disloyal, and everybody knew what that might mean. So, there was less money for everything else – including wine!

Then there was a string of poor harvests, and whilst the better-off could cope, many of our friends found it difficult to make ends meet, let alone the poor whose presence on the streets was becoming a bigger and bigger nuisance. I'm sure you'd have found a way to help, Robert. You'd have seen the bigger picture.

Then, two springs ago, I think I'd notched up your 18$^{th}$ year away from us, 'the madness' happened. Panic in the streets. The tense stand-off. The horror of the fire, and the taste of the dust and ashes that I kicked up in my desperate attempt to find anything in the remains of the burned-out castle keep that would tell me whether Jacob and Elizabeth had indeed suffered this horrible end. I burned with anger at the injustice that had been meted out on the Jewish community. Why travel to Jerusalem when there was a crusade so close at hand.

## TALES OF THE CELEBRITY HERMIT

*It was March and food supplies from a poor harvest the previous year had all but run out. Any food that was available cost at least twice as much as it would normally. But it's at times like that, that those with money to lend also had money to afford food. Don't get me wrong, everybody was suffering, but a certain group of York townsfolk decided to vent their feelings, and the Jews were an easy and obvious target.*

*I can still remember the distant but disturbing chanting as I sat exactly where I am now doing the bookwork for the business. At first, I thought it might be a wrestling match in the market place, although I quickly remembered that nothing was planned, and an impromptu gathering of that sort was highly unlikely. Then I heard children running and screaming, but not the screams of excitement, they had a haunting tone to them. Some were crying out for their parents, not knowing where to turn. I could see family groups running, and older people slipping in the muddy tracks of the town's side-roads. It seemed that the people were running without there being anyone in the chase, but when I peeped my head out of the door and looked up to a house that I knew was the home of a Jewish family, I saw cowardly thugs, running off in the other direction with anything they could lay their hands on that would fetch a decent price. I'm sure their pockets were bulging with coins and other valuables they'd managed to ransack from the house.*

*I felt sick, and immediately thought of Jacob and Elizabeth and of what might have been for Nathan, now married and with children of his own, had he not recently moved to Knaresborough. But there were plenty who had not been so fortunate. Perhaps Jacob and Elizabeth had managed to slip away and were even then walking through the fields to the west of the town making their way to join their son and family. But I was never to find out, and the home you and I once visited has been left empty ever since. An eerie, silent reminder of a people caught up in a madness fueled by jealousy, suspicion and mistrust. If only people had got to know them as real human beings.*

*In the days immediately following the madness a deathly hush fell on the town. People seemed only to be able to talk in whispers. Nothing fundamental had changed except for the fortunes of more than a handful of greedy louts who had run the other way after looting empty homes. And the blood of hundreds of people lay on the hands of the local Sheriff who had ordered the burning of the Castle keep; with men, women and children cooped up inside like cattle. But somehow the blot, and therefore the blame, seemed to be etched into everyone's conscience. I so wanted to talk to someone who might understand; but Robert, you weren't there.*

*As I remember my feelings then, it seemed impossible to hold them in, but who was I to set things right? I might have had a reasonably successful business behind me, but it was the men of the town who made the rules, meted out justice and basically ran everything. Your father felt the pain too, but we found it difficult to talk about, and I just had to hold everything in, bottled up with no release.*

*As things returned to normal, and food stocks started to be replenished, a lot of people quickly realised how dependent they had been on loans from the Jews to oil the wheels of business. Despite it being illegal, people began to find ways around the ban on charging interest. Gifts in kind was one way, a sort of bartering for the loan of some much-needed cash.*

*I'm sat here even now, with the autumn drawing in and the damp, dark evenings shortening the day, benefitting from one such gift in kind. It's a large and very warm blanket made from the best local sheep's wool and given to me for a short-term loan I made. You can't really call that usury, just doing a friend a good turn and receiving a gift to recognise it. But that's not how the Magistrates saw it. Why is it that the law looks to punish such innocent actions? Technically I may have strayed, but surely what needs to be addressed is the excess, the persistent offending that leads to exploitation, not the simple act designed to help a friend.*

*I acted, believing with every fibre of my body that the murder of so many innocent families was a great injustice that had led us to a point where difficult decisions were forced on us. And then, when no real attempt had been made to bring those who were guilty to justice, it was me who was hauled before the magistrates on a technicality.*

*There was a time, not so long ago, that I still had the energy to be angry. But now all I feel is despair, a hollowed-out suspicion that the world is out to get me at every turn. How, I ask myself, can I ever show my face to the people I once passed the time of day with. If they* were too polite to say anything, I'd know what they'd be thinking. Siminina, guilty, shamed and shunned. But my actions were innocent and well-intended! What has the world come to....?

The charge of usury came on the back of investigations into other claims against me of business irregularities, what they call 'short-measure'. I'm sure you'll realise that goods being lost in transit is not uncommon. Perhaps in this case I was somewhat foolish, but I was driven by a sense of injustice arising from the madness. You see, I think I recognised one of the men running in the opposite direction on that March day back in 1190. And, lo and behold, a year later, the family who had raised this thug came to me to buy some wine.

They lived in Beverley, which meant that a delivery had to be arranged. I can remember the feeling as my quill hovered over the invoice. I knew exactly how many barrels were on the cart, which was consistent with the order they had placed, but just adding one more to the invoice, a ghost barrel that would never be loaded on the cart, might go some way to sooth the pain, some small way of getting something back. I'd expected the family administrator to gloss over the discrepancy, it would be no skin off of his nose, and the master would get the wine he wanted. After all, that sort of thing happens all the time on the road, normally through highwaymen — but if that family had not benefitted from something far more heinous that taking from the rich to give to the poor, then I really don't know what justice is supposed to mean.

*But I got unlucky. The clerk was on the ball that day, reported it to the magistrates, and one thing led to another. How quickly can a whole life unravel before your very eyes?*

*It was a couple of weeks ago that I had my audience with the magistrates. They were very business-like. They'd been through all the books for any irregularities, hence the double charge of short measure and usury. And I couldn't deny it because the letter of the law was clear. Better to come clean and take the fine. Much easier for the rest of the family, but I came out of the court room a shattered woman.*

*Since then it seems that all I've done is to stare into this empty, dim room that was once a bustling office and storeroom. I've counted those chinks on the beam above the window may times. Sometimes I've just gazed at them, oblivious to how many there are as if the number had no significance and was melting into an infinity, an abyss of time between what I'm feeling now and what we had as a family when you were with us.*

*Robert, if this letter gets to you I want you to understand. I never meant it to turn out like this. I remember the optimism of my younger years, especially when you and Walter were growing up and showing so much promise. Walter is a real testament to the family, but firstborns always hold a special place in their mother's heart. I can't share these feelings with anyone else. Perhaps this letter will go with me to my grave, but I do feel relief in having written it.*

*I feel like I'm fading, it's an autumn feeling, and one that I'm not sure will turn to spring. I've been found out but feel that my wrongs were simply points at which well-intentioned decisions didn't fit in with the mad world around me. Was it me in the dock, or have I taken the knock for others who play the system to get away with far greater evils? I could have chosen differently but wonder if that would have left me with an even bigger sense of guilt. Guilty by not seeking to address the wrongs I saw around me, even in the small ways that became my downfall. At least I tried!*

*I do wonder what it was that drove you to those early choices that took you away from me. Should I have done something different to hold on to you, or was it God's will that you leave and find a different way, perhaps a better way? We talked about a faith in God that wouldn't end up with the enrichment of the Church when some people were still in poverty, and I think you glimpsed that possibility from the little you shared with me when you returned from Newminster Abbey. But I wonder, is such a way really to be found? Or are we all doomed to be chewed up and spat out by a world that seems hostile to simple, well intentioned actions. Can we find peace in this world, or must we wait for the next...?*

*Your loving mother,*

*Siminina*

I put the letter down on the make shift table. I felt as if I had been introduced to someone who was both intensely familiar and yet, at the same time, a stranger. Where had my mother's thoughts and feelings been hidden these recent weeks and months? Indeed, where had her regret and sense of loss when Robert left us been stored away? Should I be angry that my own mother had not confided in me? Surely, I commanded just as much respect, particularly when I'd made such a positive contribution to our family. Should I feel like the prodigal's elder brother, angry that my own parent kept this soft spot for the one who had abandoned us?

But I knew that mother was right about Robert's sense of calling. He had not left to fritter away an inheritance like the prodigal, but rather to seek out a calling in service to others. Mother seemed to know that, seemed to sense the type of life that he had chosen, even though we'd not actually heard anything over the years he'd been gone.

What should I do? What would mother have me do?

I must resolve, if at all possible, to find Robert and deliver the letter.

\*\*\*

Sometimes if you've lost something, the best way to find it is to forget about it until something pops into your head and hey presto, you remember. At first, I wondered how I would ever find my big brother, so I put the letter somewhere safe. Each morning I'd notice it by the side of my bed, but then the busyness of the day would take over.

Then a throw-away comment by a friend in the tavern caused a domino effect in my mind. There was talk about a hermit living near Knaresborough wearing the white habit of the Cistercians. Odd, except to anybody who knew Robert! And this hermit had managed to influence none other than Sir William de Stuteville to carry out a very out-of-character charitable act. I must find out more!

I obviously wanted to deliver the letter in person, and so quickly arranged things so that I could make the trip there and back in a day. As I left York at a canter, with the early spring sun on my back, my thoughts matched the sound of the horse's hooves on the track – 'was it Rob (ert)', 'was it Rob (ert)', 'was it Rob (ert)'. After just over an hour of riding we slowed to a trot, and the rhythm of my thoughts changed to match the horse's hooves once again, and I remembered mother and the letter that was in my pouch — 'mother's letter', mother's letter', 'mother's letter'.

I followed the river. It wasn't long before I smelled the smoke from a domestic fireplace, and the hint of freshly baked bread lingering in the bright but still angled rays of sunlight, playing with the smoke as it hung in layers. Then I heard a bustle of activity and was soon greeted warmly by a man looking out from a small enclosure of animals, clearly grateful to be interrupted from his mucking out. He looked like he'd seen rougher times, but his smile said that the work he was doing was welcomed, if tough.

"How do?" he said.

"Good day" I replied. "Might I find Robert nearby?"

"Well, yes, but you may have to wait a while. He'll be seeing to folk come down from Knaresborough. Always busy is Robert, unless he's praying of course, in which case you'll not rouse him at all."

As I approached the source of the lingering smoke I became aware of a small huddle, crouched by the entrance to a hut that leant against the rock face. My attention was drawn to the body language between one person dressed in a dirty white habit, who I assumed was Robert, and his visitors. There was such an intensity and a bond between the little group. They seemed to form a bubble, as if transported from another world and settled gently on the bank of the river.

When it appeared that the conversation was over, and departing gestures were being made, I approached, and Robert turned. I was close enough to catch his eyes behind the hood of his habit. There was instant recognition, and Robert opened his stance, threw back his hood and beamed at me. We hugged, and then with arms around each other's shoulders he led me down the short bank to the water side, where the noise of the river masked our conversation.

"What took you so long?" were his first teasing words. How can twenty years feel like a matter of weeks?

I don't think I actually replied to that opening remark. We exchanged glances that had clearly communicated a myriad of unspoken words, and Robert enquired knowingly, "It's mother, isn't it?"

Silently I reached for my pouch and pulled out the letter. I handed it to Robert. We embraced for several minutes, and then sank to the ground. Robert read the letter slowly. With an occasional glance my way, he drank in mother's words, and when he put the letter down in his lap his eyes turned to the skies and we prayed

– words and feelings flowed to God, and between the two of us, in that moment. Robert, just like father and I had done those few weeks ago, had been able to lay mother to rest in peace.

As we walked back up the slope to the hut Robert invited me inside. It was, as I suspected, rudimentary. What I didn't expect was the extra space that had been carved out of the rock face that the hut was leaning against. There, hidden away inside the rock, was a small altar where, Robert explained, he spent much of his time in prayer.

We discussed the nature of the work he was involved in and the labour that he and his little team did in the fields, all in aid of supporting those who fell on bad times in the town and countryside around. And when I looked again into Robert's face I could see that all this effort, and the years that had passed, had not been kind to him.

I felt proud, but also concerned for my elder brother. Proud because he was clearly living a life that was in harmony with those around him; concerned because he wasn't getting any younger. When we were small, playing in the yard or exploring the streets of York, it was Robert who looked out for me. Perhaps now it was time for me to look out for him.

I tried a couple of tacks, almost for something to say, because I could see how at peace he was in his work. I offered to find him a place in a monastery or something similar, to pay for his prayers and his living costs, to make him comfortable. But it was hardly worth suggesting when you felt the strength of the bonds he had with those around him and the place he had made his own.

In the end, I insisted on improving his current living conditions. Remembering how Robert had been fascinated as a child with the work of the masons as they fashioned stone for the Minster, and knowing that these masons were available for hire, I promised to send a group of men who could build a small chapel and extend the living space. It was the least I could do.

As I left Robert, the letter safely in his possession, I felt a sort of completion. Mother was never to know in this life that the struggles of her final weeks and months, and the questions she had asked herself, were indeed answered in some way by Robert's example. His early choices had seemed uncertain, searching, even impulsive, and it was clear that his journey to this settled position had not been smooth. But Robert seemed to have found a way, in tandem with the God that he served, to reconcile the messy world that we all contribute to with his own purpose as a human being — to worship and to serve. If only mother had lived one more year.

But regret never got anyone anywhere, and hope seemed to have knocked such feelings off their perch for Robert. As I rode back to York the rhythm of the horse's hooves gave me space to think, and to hope, that Robert's saintly example would do its work.

# Lost and Found

*Helena de Plompton*  *Nigel*

**The early 1190's**

A simple, but sumptuous feast lay before me. The harvest was going well which meant that the spread was substantial and varied – pork belly in the pot, green vegetables in abundance, cheese and fresh barley bread with its smell still lingering around the house. And autumn fruits cascading from the bowls on the table in such a way as to entice us to linger after the meat was eaten.

The large table and the open fire was at the heart of our Plompton home, open at all times to those in need, but tonight set for a special guest. Opposite me sat Robert. It was a privilege to entertain our saintly friend, and a rare thing for him to leave his disciplines, though even he allowed himself the occasional departure. He had made plans to ensure that the material rigours of his little community were carried out by his fellow workers. And we knew that on this occasion, each year, he would have been content to leave his spiritual rigours to the mercy that he knew God showed him every day, trusting that tomorrow he would wake again fresh, forgiven and energised to work.

Our special occasion tonight was to mark the anniversary of Robert's return. A return that doubled my joy, as if that were possible! You see, I had thought that my eldest, Nigel, who was now sitting at the head of the table, had been lost fighting with the King's men. Instead of which he had done what every young knight dreamt of and few achieved – he had found and married his damsel, Maria, who was sitting at the other end of the table, with one ear listening out for the children who had just been put to bed.

But my story goes back further to the time when I was the damsel. As we prepared to eat the meal before us, I remembered the tournament, as if it was yesterday.

*I heard the thundering of horses' hooves, the swoosh of noise and air as the brave knights flashed past. Snorting, rearing, turning and charging again. Victors and losers, valiant, chivalrous brothers in arms. Here was the sifting ground of the King's own men. And then I saw Peter, the sight of that sweaty, beaming, athletic form that jumped down from the handsome steed was still vivid. He'd finally earned the spurs that he'd trained so hard for. Who wouldn't have been swept off their feet!*

*I was very happy. Our five children came along in quick succession, and Nigel, the eldest adored his father. But we were not so prosperous that we could avoid the obligation to supply the King with arms when necessary, and so Peter set off – unbeknown to me, never to return...*

I gazed into Nigel's face as he exchanged banter with Robert about the day they had just spent in the fields. There was the look of his father about him, no doubt. But losing that father, now some thirty years ago, had been tough for Nigel. At the time he was not yet a man, but he was old enough to feel the loss. Peter had been the perfect dad, particularly if you inherited his ambition and enthusiasm for life. Nigel dealt with the loss by emulating all the things in his father that a little boy would be proud of. Little did he know that this ambition, and his success, would bring his mother even more heartache.

Remembering once again, it was as if history was repeating itself, but I was powerless to intervene.

*Was it really Nigel at the tournament, or was I reliving the exhilaration of seeing Peter win the prizes? I knew that Nigel needed to find his own way, and I was immensely proud of him. But when he, like his father, had gone off to join the King's men, I couldn't help but feel the double loss. I had learned to conceal the pain. Staying busy, particularly by helping others on the estate who were in need. But in the quiet moments I wondered – what if...*

Thankfully, unlike his father, Nigel had come home. And it was a homecoming that I relived every time I saw him striding up the track after a day in the fields or returning from the town after conducting some business. And today's joy was to see both my men coming down the track, Nigel's arm over Robert's shoulder, seeing them as if one.

How else could a mother feel except a sense of contentedness. I had lost my first love, and then my eldest son. Perhaps as reparation I had all but adopted another in Robert, only to see him flee. But my happiness returned when Nigel came back as if resurrected, and to add to that joy I welcomed the returning prodigal.

Even more than that. Instead of the older son complaining when the fatted calf was slaughtered, Nigel and Robert fell immediately into the sort of relationship normally reserved for brothers. Two men, one who had earned his spurs in the joust, and the other who sought a different reward, joined together in an understanding that only true brotherhood could bring.

These were the stories that we would retell around the meal table, as we did on each of these anniversaries. I had already been rewarded when Nigel and Robert entered the house that evening, having seen their beaming faces and been given a grand hug from each in turn. Maria had emerged from the bed chamber, finger at her lips but crouched and smiling as if suppressing the giggles that had no doubt been looking for a way out as she settled the children. And so, we were gathered.

Robert broke his usual convention when eating meals. For him, most mealtimes were spent in thankful silence, whilst this one would be full of spoken remembrances. We'd tell all sorts of stories, like the irreverent antics that some of the Knaresborough folk got up to when Robert visited town seeking alms, or the little triumphs we saw when people on the estate got through the tough times. But the stories would often be told with new insight or a slightly different perspective, turning each tale into something more like a play with so many actors that you never quite knew who would make their entry next.

I felt like I'd held myself all day in anticipation of the evening. The excitement of a child in an old woman's body. Maria relaxed, the smile still there, but her tiredness evident after the playful struggle to achieve the simple task of putting two children to bed. Nigel and Robert drinking long draughts of ale, quenching their thirst, and playfully competing over the aches that a hard day in the fields brought.

It was something of a tradition that Nigel prompted the first tale. "Mother", he said, "on this special anniversary, tell us again how you found this replacement son of yours", nodding playfully toward Robert. It didn't take much to bring back those memories.

*"I was missing you, of course. There you were, following in your father's footsteps off to win your spurs and rescue your damsel in distress."* I looked across to Maria who feigned a swoon. *"It was impossible to know*

where you'd got to, though I kept my ears open and listened to the town crier's news of local tournaments and distant battles whenever I could. I didn't fret. There was far too much work to do around the estate, a man's work done with a woman's common sense!" A wry and cheeky smile passed between the little group.

"Then I heard about the knight, and the hermit who served him, who were living in the area." I looked at Robert and kept the gentle stare as I told the next bit of the story. "I knew almost immediately that the knight couldn't be my own son – the circumstances would have been too bizarre. But, through this chance piece of news, I was about to be written into someone else's story. Someone I'd no reason to feel any affinity toward, but someone who would change my life."

"I remember when you walked up the path. I knew it was you from your distinctive, white habit. There had been talk in Knaresborough about how your friend the knight had returned to his home and left you to fend for yourself. Without his income, there were more visits to the town for you to seek alms. And so, to see you arrive in Plompton was no surprise. And being of good Christian stock I never sent anyone away empty handed."

"But this is where something, or someone, seemed to take over. My head was always so full of things. Things to do, things to remember, people to talk to, worries to ponder on. There was rarely a moment's peace without the busyness of the day, and sometimes of the next day, crowding back into my mind. Suddenly it was as if all this cleared and something, or someone aligned a few simple *facts. All the distractions fell away into ditches on either side of my thoughts. In between you and I came three simple images that combined into a single picture – my own private chapel of St Hilda's, the needs of some the families on the estate following a poor harvest, and your lack of a secure living since the knight had left you. Unlike him you had nobody to return to, and no belongings to speak of, so that night you spent in prayer, until dawn, in the shelter of St Hilda's."*

*"That night I lay on my back here in this house staring at the darkness above my bed wondering what it all meant. Was I being selfish, disloyal or even plain crazy to believe I'd been compensated for the losses I'd suffered? Had I simply offered you a new home, or adopted a new elder son?"*

My gaze dropped from Robert, but the moment lingered.

"Time for food." Maria broke the silence, and we all gathered around the table. We ate for a while, and as we did my mind wandered to Robert's storerooms at St Hilda's. They would be full, and the contents carefully preserved to last the coming winter and provide for any who might come across bad times. After all, you never knew whether illness, vermin or even thieves might make a family vulnerable. Thieves!

The chatter around the table continued, but I found myself taken back some five years, and in my mind's eye...

*Robert was sitting in this same kitchen repeating that word with his hands in his head. "Thieves, thieves,*

*thieves...." There was an intensity and an anger in his face as I heard how St Hilda's had been ransacked. Wanton vandalism, the food strewn across the floor and into the mud of the outside track. Completely spoilt. Useless to anyone except the scavenging rats who scurried around thinking that Christmas had come early.*

*We were both equally shocked by what had happened. We sat together through the night. Talking, praying, listening. I had urged Robert to rebuild and offered him my protection, but I knew that was of little comfort. What could a middle-aged woman with no man-about-the-house offer in the face of such attacks? Robert was preoccupied with something that Jesus had said to his disciples when they were not welcomed in their travels. 'If you are persecuted, flee to another city' He had advised. And there was nothing I could do to persuade Robert otherwise.*

*As the day dawned, instead of leaving through the kitchen door that he had come hurtling through those few hours earlier, Robert left through the front door, heading due south. Perhaps greater protection could be afforded in Spofforth in the shadow of the manor home of the Percy's. I felt I had failed. I remembered how loneliness had once filled this home, and I felt the old wounds reopened.*

"Mother." It was Nigel, noticing that I was in my own little world, and that perhaps my face was not as bright as the occasion called for. I looked at my plate, and then at the table. The mouthfuls I'd eaten paled into insignificance when I realised what a hole the men had made in the food that had been prepared. A pause in the feasting would, I thought, be welcomed. So, I looked to Robert, still half in the moment and half thinking back to his leaving, and said "Tell us again, Robert. Tell us about your prodigal time, and especially about your homecoming."

*"It wasn't an easy time," Robert said, "I know how clear things seemed to me on the night I left. My feeling of rejection drove me to actions that, whilst perhaps not regretting, certainly give me cause for thought. But I was learning something at the same time, and perhaps it's something I'm still learning. When to run, and when to stick at it, which is perhaps the hardest thing."*

We all looked at Robert as if willing him to continue his train of thought. And so, as we grazed on the fruit, Robert retold the story that was the focus of our remembrance.

*"At first I thought Spofforth was just the place to be. Living under the protection of an influential family where I could make my mark, perhaps even be an influence for good in the corridors of power. We all knew that the Percy's moved in high circles when it came to the nobility. But all that happened, unbeknown to me at first, was that people were building me a pedestal, as a sort of 'attraction' to draw the crowds. Although it felt good at first, my sense of unease grew, battling against what I thought had been a clear word from God about moving on. And so once again, that's what I had to do – move on."*

*"I was too proud to return at that point and so I sought refuge in the priory at Hedley – but once again found myself hoodwinked into believing something that turned out to be false. Perhaps I still had a certain naivety that a place like that could truly balance my calling to prayer and to the service of those in need. What I found was a self-indulgent group of escapists."*

At this point, Robert paused and bowed his head. The failure of the Church and its institutions to properly fulfil their calling, as he saw it, was a constant trouble that he felt deeply. Knowing that this could lead to certain 'overstatements' he lifted his head, shrugged his shoulders very slightly and said, gently, "I'm sorry", as if to us, but also to those he might have offended. After a brief pause Robert continued, now in a lighter mood.

*"I wasn't sure that you'd accept a prodigal back, but I did come to some sort of sense, and once again walked to your door. I don't know what I expected, particularly when I was greeted by this hulk of a man instead of your familiar face. I can remember the moment clearly"*, Robert continued, looking at Nigel, *"you were nervous, protective and not a little bemused by this monk-like figure appearing at the door. But you were quickly reassured, and then what a welcome I received!"*

*"We sat, just as we do tonight, but for the very first time. Me, wondering why I was here. You,"* looking at Nigel, *"nervous about this second prodigal. And you, dear Helena, needing once again that flash of divine guidance as you considered the little group that had gathered. What would your response be?"* Robert

*paused. "I am so grateful that you had it in your heart to welcome me again".*

Here Robert turned his body and gave his full attention and focus to me. He took my hands in his and continued.

*"On that evening when many would have considered their generosity and love to have been full-spent, you found new depths from which to draw. As if to signal what must be, you opened your heart and allowed it to create a path in your mind that defied the logic of mortals. What did this hermit on the run deserve? What new obligations had arrived on your doorstep? Surely your time, energy and commitment should be directed toward those of your own kith and kin. But as if a new source of generosity and love had been found, which instead of depleting what was available for others reinforced and invigorated it, you multiplied your generosity. I had come home."*

With those concluding words, we did what we had done each year and stood in a simple circle. Robert led us in a Psalm and a prayer for the safety of our home and of each member of the family. And after this little ceremony had concluded, we reclined at table once more.

As the evening continued I reflected on those precious memories, and on the little bundles of promise next door in the bed chamber – a new generation that would no doubt face similar challenges and choices. As for me, I regretted nothing. I married for love, and after I lost Peter I chose to manage the estate for the good of all. In what felt like pure instinct I had welcomed Robert not once, but twice. These choices did not make life easy, but the joy and contentment I felt were reward enough.

The story that had led us to this moment of warm friendship was more than simply a retelling of the facts. It reached to the heart of our beings as we sat as a close-knit family unit. The resilience and strength of this little estate, of no consequence to the powers that be whether in Knaresborough, neighbouring Spofforth, or the bustle of metropolitan York, was where true community had its beating heart. And for me, despite the challenges of life, I was content in the bosom of the family that God had guarded and guided.

# A Broken Bow

*Sir William de Stuteville*

## *During the first decade of the 13th Century*

I was a tightly strung long bow, ready at an instant to hit the target. My mind was sharp. My reach, wide. I'd ridden the changing of the royal guard from King Henry, then Richard and now to John, like a rising tide. Nobody could deflect me from a goal when I'd set my mind to it, and I travelled the highways from Lincolnshire to Northumberland as if I owned them. Northerners never took too kindly to the raping of their lands to fill the King's battle coffers – hard graft rewarded by swingeing taxes. But if you kept your senses and your legal wits about you, there was always a way to come out on top. And I'd pretty much managed that all my life.

To crown of all my conquests, I had been made Sheriff of Yorkshire, a 'full house' to trump anyone on the gaming table. Which also gave my trips between Lincoln and Roxborough a convenient stop-off point at the Percy's home. Now there's a family that's going places, I would say. Great location in Knaresborough Forest. Perfect for hunting, and for keeping the King happy by way of the fines we charged when the locals stepped out of line.

It was after one such hunting trip at Knaresborough Castle that I finally over-strung the long bow, and it came about in a way that was completely unexpected.

I always enjoyed a bit of a feast. The boar was on the spit, the wine was flowing, and the hunting dogs were lounging around in anticipation of the bones that would be thrown their way as the evening progressed. It had been a day of relatively uneventful hunting. The best of the season had passed, and the days were short, something I was secretly glad of given my advancing years. But I was still a proud and upright rider, always up for a short gallop, using my cunning rather than brute force to outflank the younger knights. Cunning was always something I looked for in the up and coming generation – a bit of guile and the ability to scheme.

And so, thinking I'd test the young knights at the feast, I threw out a challenge. "For King and Country", I shouted above the revelling, "what did you see today that shows how our Forest laws need to be driven home with new energy?" There was a pregnant pause.

Perhaps I'd asked the question too early in the evening before the wine had taken its effect. Or perhaps they thought it was a trick question. My reputation for attention to detail and my legal prowess was renowned after all. So, I bellowed "what about the smoke we saw on the way back to the castle? What d'you find at the bottom of a column of smoke?" Clearly not wanting to state the obvious, the lily-livered whipper snappers stayed quiet.

Almost losing my temper I told 'em what I'd expect to find. "Vagabonds. Thieves. Scoundrels. And a royal beast cooking on their spit. Thieved. Nicked. Plundered from the King's Forest larder." The tension was rising, but I was determined to hammer my point home, and to get some sort of grit and backbone in response to my challenge.

Then I heard some murmuring from the back of the room. "Speak up", I bellowed. "What've you got to say for yourself? What ingenious way of filling the Sheriff's coffers have you come up with?" It was Nigel de Plompton who spoke. I knew him from previous hunting trips. Well regarded locally, but this was a family that was never going to come to anything. Too much female influence, and a poor reflection of their neighbours, the Percy's.

Nigel spoke. "Sir William, I think you are referring to Robert, a saintly man if you remember, who lives across the river from the Forest. You moved him on from Rudfarlington some 7 years ago."

The smug, patronising response was typical of his sort. I instantly disliked anyone who addressed me without an appropriate level of fear and trembling – and I certainly had my doubts about this man Robert's holy credentials. He was part of no formal order, didn't bow the knee to either church or state, and was therefore pretty much useless to anyone. A parasite on the land.

I ignored the small detail that Robert was now across the river from the Forest. There were still plenty of opportunities for him to trespass. And I was not about to release the pressure on these weak brothers in arms! "Am I hearing the same reluctance to act against this man as last time? Surely someone is willing to rid the Forest of this vermin once and for all..." It was a dangerous strategy, but they were sticking together in silence. Unless I picked on someone at random then they clearly felt that there was safety in numbers. I decided to take the matter into my own capable hands – nothing would slip through my fingers.

I stood facing de Plompton, but scanning the whole room, and thumped the table so hard that the plates jumped and clattered. "I swear on the Bible that before tomorrow is out I will have personally, and permanently, rid this place of that thieving imposter, Robert." And as I said the name I motioned with my hand as if I was thrusting my fist into the mouth of a lion to tear out its tongue. Before sitting down, and to ensure the matter could be laid to rest, I gave my instruction, "and I expect every one of you to be ready to ride out and witness the act at dawn." I sat down heavily.

Not wanting to prolong the silence, I called for more wine, slapped a few backs that were in my reach and changed the subject.

After the dogs had done their work cleaning up the remains of our feast it was time to retire. Many of the knights simply lay back on the cushions and rugs scattered in the enclaves of the room. The fire that had served us up some tasty pork now provided warmth for the night. I left the ragged ends of an evening of feasting to enter the King's chamber – always a pleasure, and a pity not to make use of it when not otherwise occupied.

I never had any problem going to sleep. Conscience rarely troubled me, and the wine would do its work. After relieving myself in the royal wardrobe I climbed onto the Kings' four-poster, snuffed out the oil lamp and lay flat out on my back, embracing the soporific effects that exercise, good food and alcohol brought. I was vaguely aware that I was snoring, and then – dreamland.

I shudder now when I remember the nightmare that followed. Never before had I felt so helpless. If I were to face the same horrors when awake then I could put up a fight, but I was prone and helpless. I wanted to rise, but the nightmare held me fast and I was powerless against the horrors that filled my head.

In the distance, but rapidly approaching, I saw a ball of fire. It swerved and banked as if out of control. As it approached me I could see that the fire was coming from an iron chariot, or perhaps it was a sledge as I could see no wheels. It was being dragged through the air by two athletic and muscular men, but even they were finding it difficult to control the fiendishly constructed weapon. They were working their hardest, sweat pouring down their faces from the heat and the exertion, but even they were having difficulty in avoiding the pitch-forks that were protruding, and rotating viciously, intent on doing maximum damage to whatever got in its way.

And what was in its way was my own exposed side. I'd lost the sense of time in the middle of a nightmare of noise and fury. It was as if I could feel the penetrating assault of the fiery iron whilst also looking in horror at the sight of the on-coming onslaught – the now and the not yet of anticipated doom held in horrible tension.

But worse was to come. As if the two men who were about to launch their lethal, flaming weapon at me was not enough, a third man, perhaps 10-foot-tall, rose at the foot of my bed. He rushed at me swinging weapons the likes of which I'd never seen even at the roughest and most brutal of tournaments. I was being challenged to single combat, something that I had never shrunk from before, but I felt a strange sense of helplessness. I was motionless, knowing that whatever I did could neither deflect the oncoming fiery weapon or give defence against the deathly thud of the frontal assault.

Amongst all this fury and fire invading my mind in the timelessness of my dream, there came words of accusation and challenge from my assailant. It was a challenge for the right to carry out my solemn vow against St Robert. "Get up, take up your mace, defend your own neck. Back-up your claim to mete out justice to those weaker than yourself."

And then another voice emerged from the depths of my own unconscious state, a voice so firm and sure that even though it seemed like an echo it had a strong ring of confidence. And the words I heard were those from seven years ago, relayed by the knights returning from Robert's cave. "I am not afraid" – something I'd scoffed at when uttered in pointless defiance from such an insignificant. "The Lord is my protector" – once again, words that had seemed meaningless when I was Lord of much of the East and North of England! But these echoes, coming as if from another realm, had greater solidity than anything I seemed to be able to muster in the helplessness of the onslaught in my dream.

In the face of an assault on my left flank, and the full-frontal challenge to combat, I rolled over in submission. It was my only choice. I battled it at first, but the tightly strung bow would finally have to snap in submission. I had nothing left to fire, and in that moment, I knew that I was the penitent.

I woke with a start, but also with the realisation that I had rolled on to my side and was now looking precariously over the edge of the bed – I held myself, wondering about what had just happened. Could I brush it aside? As I entertained the thought of simply rolling over again and forgetting all about it the vivid nature of the dream grew in my now waking consciousness. I faced a choice, now fully conscious, that would bind me forever.

But what was I thinking. William de Stuteville never gave in so easy. It was just a dream after all. I'd lose face. But there was a force behind what I'd seen and experienced that I couldn't deny. The bravado I'd normally rely on had simply evaporated – and whether a dream or not, the experience still felt real. The challenge remained fresh as I moved from sleep to consciousness, and I still felt committed to the decision to lay down arms and submit.

Aware that I was still hovering on the edge of the bed, and as if translating the mental submission into a physical act, I moved my legs from under the blankets so that they lowered me onto the floor, knees first. Yesterday, like all the days before it, I would have strode out of my bed chamber to face the day intent on asserting my power and influence at all costs. But now I was to start this new day from a position of humility. I prayed, not something I normally did without a member of the clergy reading the words. But this was a prayer that had to be in my own words – a solemn promise from one who knew that their own power and influence had been surpassed. I had reckoned that I was faring well in the 'royal stakes', but now had to come to terms with a new reality, previously hidden, but ever present.

Having been woken by my nightmare before dawn I had time to think about Robert. There was one task for today, though it would be hard – I was not in the habit of climbing down. But what would it mean beyond today's delicate situation? I could only wonder. Perhaps, if I was strong enough to ask advice from the one that I'd previously taunted and railed against, then I'd start to find out. I heard the cock crow.

I was accustomed to early starts and was often in the saddle soon after dawn to make good progress on my travels. But my trip today would be short, though hugely significant. I ate a little whilst those who had feasted the night before were in various stages of rising. I could see that some were gathered in small huddles, no doubt discussing what might happen when we set off for our rendezvous with Robert.

There was a bit of time to make plans, and I felt that my change of heart needed to be demonstrated by action. I therefore called in the senior administrator who kept the records of land ownership in the area and checked what livestock the estate had in its gift. When I emerged from this early morning consultation the others were ready, but I kept my cards close to my chest. After all, I was still working things out – perhaps I expected some sort of divine guidance as we approached my erstwhile enemy, although I wasn't sure I'd know what that looked or sounded like.

The procession of knights along the riverside that morning must have seemed a sober affair. There was little conversation, which was unusual given the gentle pace. As we got close I sent de Plompton ahead – I guessed he would know exactly where to find Robert, and how to break the news that the Sheriff was on his way. I still gave little away, but when we saw Robert ahead of us, with Nigel just a step or two behind and Robert's little band of followers visible in the background, I signalled the dismount. The thudding of a dozen or so burly men onto the soft leafy ground, and the snorting of horses, briefly disturbed the tranquility of the river side.

The fact that I made no lunge toward Robert kept the situation calm, if tense. As far as those with me were concerned all options were open, and the inevitable, however I chose to execute it, was now only a matter of time. I could hear whispers from behind me, perhaps speculating about what game I would play to teach everyone a lesson. But the Sir William that these knights knew from the previous evening had been disarmed.

I looked Robert up and down. I was dumbfounded that it was this man's words of gentle but firm defiance that had been my undoing. Words that had lodged unknowingly in my mind, the mind of one of the most powerful men in England, only to come back and haunt me. I could see no army surrounding or backing up the robed and saintly figure, but he remained so sure of his calling, and so in tune with the backcloth of river, woodland and band of followers, that it was as if he was rooted into the very fabric of the place. Firm. Unmoving. The sense of helplessness that had come over me in my dream now took on a different guise. I knew now that any physical assault on the place that Robert held would be as useless and pitiful as rising to face my assailants in the night. But the feeling of helplessness gave me a strange reassurance that what I was about to do was, indeed, the right and only choice open to me.

There were about 20 paces between myself and Robert, close enough to see each other's faces clearly.

But I did not advance. I signalled to Nigel to come and take the reins of my horse and hold him steady. There was another pause. And then, taking just two steps forward, I sank to my knees for the second time that day and looked at the earth in front of me. It felt longer than it probably was, but after a few moments I heard the hem of Roberts habit brushing the early autumn leaves as he approached me. And then, in silence, he laid his hand on my head. I uttered words I never thought I'd say, and that those gathered must have heard with utter incredulity.

"Robert", I said, "you are loved by a greater Lord than I, and so I ask your forgiveness for the wrongs I have done you." After a brief pause, Robert crouched in front of me and we looked into each other's faces. I described what I had seen and heard overnight. It was not easy for me to relive the horror of my nightmare, but it seemed appropriate to acknowledge the nature of my ordeal and the reason for my penance. As soon as I had finished, almost before my final words, Robert was praying out loud. "May God grant you peace" were his final words, and the kiss of peace his final act before we rose as one to face the surprised onlookers.

I wasn't used to smiling, but it was apparently remarked on in the stories that circulated of that morning's events that my face was beaming as I rose. Not knowing exactly how things were going to turn out I had only a half-formed set of words to offer the incredulous gathering. But I was confident in my new-found philanthropy, not that it would buy me anything, but that it was the right thing to do. Here, in Robert, I had found the right channel for the work of a new Lord. Work that had already shown that it could stand the test of time. Now, I hoped, establishing Robert formally in the estate rolls would mean an even greater ability to carry out this work.

Land and the means to till that land was granted, as well as alms with which Robert could support the needy on a regular basis. And in a parting shot, having made my little speech, I took the reins of my horse back from Nigel and nodded knowingly toward him saying "and I'm confident I can leave the paperwork for you to deal with Nigel." It was probably as close to a second apology as I could muster for one morning, but there was an understanding that passed between us as I urged my body back onto my horse to make the return journey to the Castle.

# Flashes of Hope

*The townsfolk of Knaresborough*

## *Reflecting Robert's life from the early 1190's to his death*

What is it that makes me, a Jew, want to write down stories about a Christian holy man in the hope that someday he would be recognised for what he truly is – a saint? I'd be a rich man if I had a silver penny for every time I was asked that question. But Robert was my childhood friend, and it seemed as if God's hand was guiding our respective journeys through life.

# PETER LACEY

When we played together as boys in the streets of York nothing mattered except our friendship. We had very different backgrounds. Like many Jews, my family were encouraged to cross the channel, initially by William and then by those who followed, to support their conquests by using our skills in financial management. Someone had to keep the Royal show on the road, and I'm not sure there were many others who the Kings of England trusted. Robert's family on the other hand had strong Northern roots and had come good through hard graft. But our families found common cause in the commerce of York, and so we became very close.

We lost touch when Robert left to follow his religious calling. I could see it coming. I remember one occasion when we were about 15, the age at which boys usually spent their time talking about girls. We were sat in one of our favourite spots, just outside the mason's yard next to the Minster. The workmen had gone home, and dusk was falling. We'd need to be on our way home soon, so it was a surprise when Robert said, '*if only people could be shaped to fit so snuggly together like those stones – that would be a better world, wouldn't it?* Knowing there was no short answer we simply looked at each for a few minutes, and then, to break the silence, I jumped up and said, 'race you to the corner'. So, we sprinted off in the direction of our homes, straining to be first to the corner where our paths would separate.

But those words stayed with me. I had no idea that it would become such a driving force in his life, as I have discovered all these years later when our paths crossed again in the place I had made home, Knaresborough.

I had come to love my adopted town, although it was far from being an idyll! You might call it 'honest', a sort of matter of fact friendly. Hospitable, without the frills. It was a relatively new town, with activity and trade focused on the castle.

And it was an impressive castle. Sure, there were risks of invasion from the Scots, although we were hardly on the front line. And then there was the need to impress the locals to avoid any uprising when times were hard. But you got the distinct impression that the location of the castle was as much about its suitability as a grand hunting lodge, and, of course, for the views, as about defence.

And what views they were. The river sparkled through the canopy of mixed woodland trees. Every day could be a different season, and the colours were often magnificent. Looking upstream you'd glimpse the spire of St Mary's Church; across the river the ground rose gradually toward the moors and to the quality hunting that kept many of the townsfolk in work – as it also kept them on edge in case the forest laws were broken, even inadvertently.

We, like many others, had been welcomed, no questions asked. I had decided that I would use my skills in the more delicate aspects of metal work – weapons needed to look good, and horse regalia said something about the station of a man. So, I set up my workshop a few hundred yards from the castle wall and earned an honest living.

Looking after a growing family can take all your energy, which is how it was for many years after our move from York. People would come and go, and stories about everyday folk would waft through the ale houses, between the tradesmen and at the riverside on washday, tales that would be told later around the fireplace at home. These stories settled into the recesses of my mind as if of no consequence, but they were doing their work, as I now realised.

As our children grew, and my skills in metalwork became more refined – which was just as well because the body can only take so much heavy anvil work – I found myself becoming more attuned and more sensitised to the stories I heard. Rough stones grating, or even sparking off each other with life's ups and downs.

I began to sense undercurrents that would catch people unaware, off guard, unprepared. Sometimes people would stumble; a few weeks of hardship after an illness, or a loss through accident or theft. On some occasions, just a small misadventure would cause people to spiral out of control. Nothing seemed to be able to stop the fall. Many of us would help in whatever ways we could, but some were too embarrassed to ask until it was too late. And what could one man, one family, achieve anyway?

Our children mixed freely. We were particularly proud of our eldest, Jacob, named after his grandfather and born within a year of the madness that ended the lives of so many of our community in York. He, of course, knew nothing of those days and the heartache it had caused.

We lived in fear for several months after the massacre, not knowing if we'd need to flee further from home or could settle in safety. But settle we did, and thankfully the madness didn't spread.

Just like me when I was a boy, Jacob had a few special friends rather than running with the crowd. And the world was too small not to make friends from all walks of life. And so it was that Jacob and a local lad called Philip had become inseparable. This brought back memories that had been shrouded by the passage of time, two young boys gazing up at the castle as it was being fortified, just like Robert and I had looked on the Minster a generation ago.

But then something changed. Innocence and wonder at the strength of the castle became a foreboding and a dread on Phillip's face. The boys avoided their usual haunts and spent more time away from the town. This lasted a couple of weeks, until one night when Jacob came to us after a fishing trip with Phillip. I looked at him and asked playfully, 'What, caught nothing today?' He looked a little sheepish and shook his head. Missing out on a catch had never been such a serious matter before. I probed a little, trying to lift his mood. 'Come on', I said, 'mother's got a stew in the pot. No need to worry.' But it didn't change Jacob's mood and after a brief pause he said, 'It's Phillip. He didn't catch anything either. And if he goes home without something to eat for the family they'll go hungry again.'

'Again?', I said. 'What do you mean, again?' At that moment, Jacob took half a look behind him and beckoned with his hand for Phillip to come in from the shadow. 'Phillip's dad has been put in jail. And it's for nothing,' Jacob said between gritted teeth. And it's been two weeks now, and there's no food in the house and they don't know when, or if, his dad will come out again.'

By this stage, Lydia had come to join the little group and looked at me anxiously. Such stories were common, but this time it was standing on our family threshold. What should we do? How could we help? We did the obvious and the immediate and sent Phillip home with enough for a family meal, and a bit more to tide them over. But once the children were in bed Lydia and I sat wondering what we should do now that we were confronted by such a need. How could we support Jacob, who clearly felt Phillip's pain? We had to think into Phillip's situation. A good Christian family would surely seek out spiritual help, and perhaps find comfort that way, but being Jews, we had few links in that direction. If it was really that bad then alms could be provided from the Church, although family pride and embarrassment could be a hurdle. We went to bed troubled, but with the start of a plan in our minds.

As Jews, we were obviously free from the obligations of Church attendance. But that also meant that we had little to go on when it came to finding the best way to help Phillip's family. We had, however, heard about a monk, or was he a hermit? – these terms never meant a lot to us – who might be able to help. So, the next day, instead of heading down the hill on one side of the town toward St Mary's, I headed in the opposite direction.

I walked briskly, not knowing exactly where the hermit would be found. But it was as if the track knew the feet of someone in need, or at least of someone carrying another man's need. After about 20 minutes I heard voices, people working the land in a clearing on the side of the river. I approached, and after allowing for the time it took to down tools, stretch backs and take a few steps toward me, I was greeted warmly.

'Eh up!' they said. 'you lookin' for Robert?'

Robert? A thought flashed through my mind but settled again quickly in the shadows. 'I'm looking for a hermit who I've heard may be able to help a friend of mine.'

'That'll be Robert, then,' came the reply, 'you've come a smidgen too far, but if you turn around and head down to the river you'll find 'im there.' The thought rushed back into my mind. Could it be?

When you're up close to someone there are few faces that you wouldn't recognise, even with an extra 20 or 30 years etched on their brow. I simply didn't know what to say. Thoughts of Phillip's family completely left me for what seemed like an age but was probably only a few minutes. Rather than being surprised, though, Robert appeared almost relieved. More than relieved, released. I saw tears in his eyes. Robert spoke first.

'Nathan, you're alive. For all these years I've not known whether, or how, to mourn for such a close friend. We are guilty of a great harm to your people, something I confess to God on a regular basis. Whilst there is peace from those prayers, there are also echoes of such atrocities in what I see around me. Distrust, jealousy, fear. They are still the drivers of so much evil. There is such a burden, a weight in the world that only God can lift, but it's hard'.

I sensed in Robert the same insight and the same ambition that I witnessed so many years ago. Wanting to see people built into an edifice that would bring glory to God, only to experience the challenges that such a vision brought with it. I was eager to hear the whole story from the time we parted to this very moment. But first I had just a snippet of my own story to tell.

Robert made an attempt to lighten the mood. 'So', he asked, 'what brings you to my door? Have you decided to convert?' There was a cheeky grin on his face when he said that! Whilst I managed a brief grin my mood remained sombre. 'Something more immediate than the eternal state of my soul I'm afraid', I replied. 'There's a family in need, and I know it's one of many, but…', I paused, thinking about whether I needed to justify my plea on behalf of Phillip's family. Surely there were many families like this? I wondered if I was wasting my time and Robert's. Whatever happened would be a drop in the ocean compared to the extent of suffering and injustice I saw on a regular basis. But Phillip was Jacob's friend, and I thought about the hurt that he clearly felt.

'I don't know the details, Robert, but there's a family that our eldest is friendly with and the father is in prison. I know he's not the sort to deliberately step outside the law and suspect there's a technicality – but it's hurting his family. Badly. It just shouldn't be like this.'

That set off a whole trail of events, too detailed and mangled in my memory to recall, but together, Robert and I found what was needed to feed the family, we brought the case to the attention of the local magistrate, prepared the papers for an early hearing and got a date for Phillip's release.

I'd never done anything like that before. Working with Robert felt like putting my hand back into a well-worn glove. Except this time, we were in business, no longer talking about our aspirations and sorting out the world's problems from a comfortable distance. This was tough, and it was real. And that's where the image of those stones came back.

As we helped Phillip's family get back on their feet I was introduced to others who had been helped by Robert. How did I miss these little pockets of hope? I suppose our Jewish faith gave us a secure and close-knit community, a bit like a bubble that Jacob had now burst! I began to realise why the track down to Robert's cave was so well trod. I could never permanently cross the boundary that divided our two communities, but the door was now open for visitors. As an outsider, I could take a dispassionate view. Word of mouth is fine, but stories carried along by hearsay don't have the same lasting power. Who would capture for posterity the good that Robert was doing?

And that's what made me decide. I would become the chronicler of Robert's work, and the impact he made on the lives of those he called 'the people of the tower'. Phillip's family gave me my calling card. Unbeknown to me, and clearly a matter of some interest amongst the locals, word was circulating that there was a Jewish family in town who had put themselves out for a good Christian family. I didn't need to look far for more examples.

Flicking through the parchments that I now have in front of me, people jump off the page. One middle-aged woman came and sat next to me when there were others waiting to see Robert, which was not an uncommon thing. Elizabeth, she said her name was, and she had come simply to say thank you to Robert. She'd been clearing out a room at home and came across some buttons from her ex-husbands coat, saved in case they were useful at some point, but carrying a weight of emotion beyond their simple function. Finding them again had brought back the memories of the words that Robert had shared with her during her time of mourning. Words from scripture, words of comfort that saw her through the dark times. 'I just had to come down to say thank you again to dear Robert', she told me.

But the stories weren't all tales of smooth sailing, and Robert didn't shy away from what you might call 'the difficult cases'. One story was particularly hard to write, coming from one of the labourers working Robert's land to provide for those in need. His name was John, and I can remember him telling me his story.

'You might say I was feral. Delusions of emulating Robin Hood but sinking quickly into robbing the rich to keep myself alive. It all started back in York where I grew up. I'd been left to run the streets and was often in trouble. Petty little things, basically being a nuisance. It made me feel noticed. When the madness happened, I was up for the game, thinking nothing of stuffing my pockets full of goodies as the Jews were rounded up.'

At that point John paused, suddenly realising what he'd said.

'I am very ashamed of what I did Nathan, that's the honest truth. And Robert has assured me that there is forgiveness in Christ.' I nodded. He paused for a moment and stood. I wondered whether that was to be the end of the story, but he motioned for me to stay. I watched him enter a nearby hut, which I assumed to be his accommodation, and he returned with his hand closed around an object. Sitting down next to me again he opened his hand and said, 'you'll know what this is then.' To my surprise, I saw a mezuzah, one of the little boxes containing words of scripture that would have been fixed to the doorframe of each Jewish home in York. 'I tore it off the door of one of the houses. I don't know why. It had no monetary value. It was more like a trophy to say I'd been there. To show off to the other boys on the street'.

'York wasn't a nice place to be after that night', John had continued. Which is when I found myself caught up in the world of outlaws. Living on the fringe. Not in the forest you understand, that would have been far too risky. And the Great North Road was beyond us in terms of the calibre of people travelling and the body guards they used to protect their valuables. We lived in the in-between. Petty thieving, rarely noticed, lying low, never a nuisance for long before we moved on. That was our life. Carrying everything we had in our pouches – heaven knows why the mezuzah stayed with me, but it's small enough, and however rough my upbringing had been, it reminded me of the only home I knew. Touching the little object reassured me that I did have roots somewhere, which I suppose is what it would have done for the original owner.'

I was surprised at the insight John had, but then remembered that he'd been working alongside Robert for a good number of years. Plenty of time for these things to rub off on a willing learner.

He continued his story. 'We just about made it through our first winter in the wild, but then things got really tough. Illness took its toll, and arguments became more frequent. We were living more and more dangerously just to survive, and it was clear we'd need to disband. I couldn't go back to York. There were people there who didn't like me. And so, it just felt easiest to go to the nearest town where there was the possibility of picking up some scraps to live on. I was never going to be a credit to my new home of Knaresborough. Sleeping rough, picking up odd jobs, still prone to misbehave.'

'One or two people did look out for me, in a good way that is. But I was never able to repay them. I was the proverbial bad penny. And that's the state in which Robert found me, bouncing around from one little crisis to the next, teetering on the edge, ready to fall off at the slightest misfortune. I think somebody must have mentioned me to Robert. When he found me, and we chatted over a bowl of soup in a local tavern, nothing I could say seemed to impress or alarm him. At the end of our meal he simply invited me to come and do some honest labour in return for a bed, and food enough to keep body and soul together. It didn't feel like I had much option.'

'It didn't work out well at first. I'd forgotten, if I ever really knew, what a day's labour felt like. I was troubled at nights with haunting images from my past, and the allure of the woods were strong. There'd be times when I'd disappear for a couple of days, only to come to my senses, listen to my belly, and return sheepishly to my hut. There were no punishments, apart from increased expectations of me to follow Robert's disciplines even more closely. Something that strangely I wanted to do, if only I could summon the strength.'

'I think it was people like me, if I'm not bragging, that got Robert the reputation of harbouring thieves, which I suppose was true. But Robert never saw me as such, and gradually I turned my life around.'

As I reflected on his story, which was certainly not an instant miracle of the sort you'd read in the Christian scriptures, I nonetheless realised the marvel of how Robert had worked with John. I knew that a lot of prayer had been offered for him even before he realised that something spiritual was transforming his life. This was an important story to capture for posterity.

There were other stories too, like Emma's. So many knocks in her life. She was encouraged to seek help from Robert by her friends whilst in an advanced state of melancholy. Once again, the miracle worked slowly, but work it did. Many was the time when Robert would look her out on his visits to the town, seeking alms and giving spiritual succour in the same visit. It's a real testament to Robert's saintly life to see Emma now amongst her friends, renewed by the hope that Robert had instilled in her and sustained by his continued prayers.

And then there was Thomas. A fine upstanding member of the town in his younger years, but now struggling to find his place. Robert was such an astute observer and intense listener that he could discern people's inner disposition and attend to any spirit of pride before restoring them to a proper sense of their spiritual standing before God. A standing that was dowsed with love from on high, but that nonetheless demanded a choice.

Every story was different. It amazed me how Robert's work had been invisible to me, until I became unwittingly part of someone else's pain. But once that door opened I had entered a world of both distress and hope, jumbled together like garments in a wash basket. Each item discarded until someone took the care and attention needed to refresh a life and make it fit for wearing again. I didn't know a lot about sainthood, but when I thought about some of the stories from the Jewish scriptures then surely Robert was a Holy man, a man of real faith, a saint in any other language.

But there was something else that happened when Robert did his work. He was the mason, and there was a building being fashioned out of stones previously rejected. I reminded him once of what he had said those many years ago at York Minster, and how I felt it truly had been reflected in his life's work. He smiled when I mentioned it, a knowing smile that passed through his whole body as if settling the agitation and constant striving that drove him on.

He clearly felt a degree of satisfaction that he had been faithful to his calling, and to hear that acknowledged by a friend meant a lot to him. It was also, from what I remember, the only time when Robert tried to convert me. The words still buzz around in my head, a quote from the Christian scriptures that I also recognised from the Hebrew Bible, although it was now clearly impregnated with new meaning in Robert's life, that *'As you come to him, the living Stone, rejected by humans but chosen by God and precious to him, you also, like living stones, are being built into a spiritual house to be a holy priesthood, offering spiritual sacrifices acceptable to God through Jesus Christ'.*

# A Clash of Kingdoms

*Sir Brian L'Isle*    *King John*

## 1216

Who would have thought that my chosen career as a household administrator would involve me witnessing the clash of two mighty kingdoms! Given the times we're in you might expect such a clash to include death and awe, but this was a different sort of power struggle.

The location and circumstances of the encounter may not at first appear to justify such a claim. It was on the riverbank in a gently wooded part of northern England. Two men stood face to face in a moment pregnant with meaning. Both were old, and their age had refined and sharpened the intent with which they pursued their respective goals. It was more like an arm wrestle than a gladiatorial contest. But the stakes were high, and their advanced years meant that they were more, not less, prepared for the face-off. Here was John, King of England, and the saintly Robert. Why the high stakes? You'll need to come on the journey to understand that.

As a younger man, I had been apprenticed as administrator to one of the larger houses in Aldborough. The stories that circled around that historic settlement fascinated me, and when it came to the passing of kingdoms the stones of that place could surely have told some tales! According to the fireside yarns it had been the centre of the Celtic tribe of the Briganti. They had been such formidable foes for the Romans, but the legionaries triumphed and so it became an important river crossing, on Dere Street heading north from York.

I became enthralled by the big canvas on which history is written. In the early days of my career I often saw the impact of momentous events. They might be acted out in the politics and battlefields of Europe, but they rippled down into my daily responsibilities. My job, you see, was in the details of estate management. And that included: ensuring the tax affairs were in order; that the household was well supplied with food; that the horses were cared for; that equipment and building materials were available whenever needed; and whatever else was necessary to keep the place in order. If forays to the continent to restore our Norman overlord's territories went badly, then new ways of raising money for the King, and the consequent inflationary impact, would follow each other as surely as night follows day.

The affairs of state were a distant, but intriguing fascination for me. But they receded after my chance meeting with Robert, a saintly man living near Knaresborough. In later years, he told me that he had prayed for a helper, and that when our paths crossed whilst I was visiting the town to enquire about a new supply of game, he had felt a strong sense that I was the answer to his prayer. You wonder sometimes whether God should've let both parties know, but perhaps I wasn't listening.

Apparently, he'd been watching as I bartered in the market. As I was leaving I heard a voice from under the hood of his habit, "Follow me, and I will make you a steward of the Lord and Saviour". I checked in case there was someone else nearby, but no, he was addressing me. It wasn't as if I was even looking for a new position, but something told me I should listen.

We spent that evening on what seemed like an extended interview, although instead of checking my credentials he was intent on describing the vision he had for the little community he was building, just a mile away alongside the river. Chief amongst the community's needs was a competent administrator who could relieve him of that burden, meaning that he could devote more time to prayer and to comforting those in need. Getting a new position is normally done by recommendation, but Robert was adamant that the recommendation had come from the best of sources! We didn't exactly discuss terms either. I was simply assured that I would receive everything I needed.

Before we parted that evening, I had given my commitment to Robert. It'd be a new adventure. I'd have to work my notice, but I was already apprenticing the next steward in the household, and there needed to be some sort of career progression, if you could call working in what I understood to be a religious community as that!

The first year with Robert was like being birthed into a whole new world. I'd come with what I thought would be the necessary tools of the trade and a small collection of my own personal belongings. Quills, ink, parchments, pouches to keep the papers dry, abacus and a few personal documents from Aldborough. Then there were clothes for different occasions. But even the meagre baggage I brought seemed too much for the lifestyle expected of me. Robert took great care in the early weeks and months to instruct and encourage me. Inevitably, this early attention could not be sustained, and the book keeping that was necessary as the crops were harvested and then put into storage was considerable.

I remember the low point. It was after the main crop was safely put away and I had more time on my hands and less to think about. That's when the doubts really started flooding in. What on earth was I doing here? The comforts and privileges of being chief steward in a modest estate begged me to return. But my job had been taken by another. I felt like a cog that didn't quite fit in. What I had known as cast iron rules of bookkeeping and household management were interpreted by Robert as guidance to serve a greater good, and there didn't seem to be a handbook for that. And so, as the autumn drew in and the days grew shorter, I slid into a quiet and melancholy mood.

Nights were the worst. I still hadn't got used to the scratchy blankets and straw bedding, which meant that sometimes I simply lay churning thoughts over in my head, drifting between dreams and semi-consciousness, never really knowing where the boundary lay. I convinced myself that I had nothing in common with Robert's little band. There was nobody who understood, and even Robert was pre-occupied with other people's needs now. It was on a night like this, as soon as there was enough light to see by, that I raised myself and walked away.

I felt in a stupor, stumbling a little from lack of sleep, not as careful as I might have been about disturbing others. My mind was on other things. The path I took was unfamiliar, although I'd set off in the general direction of York. I felt I needed the anonymity that such a place would give me. An early autumn storm had brought down several branches that blocked my way causing me to leave the path on occasion, and the mud hidden under the fallen leaves started to add weight to the bottom of my robe.

I stumbled along, tired and preoccupied, hampered by the conditions but wanting to make swift progress away from what I'd convinced myself was all just a bad mistake. But then I tripped and fell heavily. I remember cursing at myself as I lay in the mud, can I possibly fall any lower!

My first attempt to stand told me that my leg was badly hurt. What a fool, I thought. Struggling against the thorny bushes that tugged at my clothes I dragged myself to the nearest tree and managed to lean against it, legs outstretched but not daring to look at the damage. I shivered. Feeling a little faint, I tried to focus on the situation. There was little I could do but sit, fighting against what would have been a very unmanly sob.

Then I heard someone coming. Peering through the bushes I could sense it was a lone traveller, although I couldn't raise myself sufficiently to see. Perhaps this was a good Samaritan who would patch me up and send me on my way. But when the figure came around the corner into full view I looked up and, to my surprise, it was Robert. My flight from the little camp had clearly not been as stealthy as I'd imagined.

Instead of looking concerned he was smiling, perhaps even with the suggestion of a gentle giggle being held back. This was not in keeping with my predicament. I was cross. "What about that sermon you're always preaching about laughing with those who laugh and crying with those who cry?", I said. But he parried like a skilled swordsman, Bible quote for Bible quote, and replied "No man who looks back after putting his hand to the plough is worthy of the Kingdom of God." And then we both laughed, although it hurt! Who'd have thought only a year ago that I'd have been quoting scripture to a devoted and spiritual man such as Robert, and yet here we were trading Bible quotes, as if sparring. He knelt in front of me, still smiling but with a concerned expression as his eyes looked me up and down.

And in those eyes, was a question. The unavoidable question in the situation we found ourselves in. It could be expressed in different ways, 'Are you really leaving, Yvo?', or 'Won't you come home', or even 'Do you love me?'

I didn't really understand the process that brought Robert and I to an embrace that answered all those questions, and more. It wasn't a decision that relied on a rational thought process, but neither was it irrational. It was, after all, the seeming logic of my perceived predicament as Robert's steward that had played on my mind so much and landed me in this mess in the first place. Rather, this was a decision based on a combination of intuition and the evidence of Robert's daily life. What I'd observed in him clearly worked at a different level, a more important level than the logical. People's lives were what mattered to Robert, and somehow, without words, that's what he communicated to me as we sat in the mud.

I knew then, despite my previous doubts, that this partnership would last. Indeed, that we had passed over some sort of rubicon from which there was no turning back. Robert knelt to address my injury, and his healing hands did their work. Within the hour, we were back at the cave.

I was keen to demonstrate my change of heart in a meaningful way. I knew that Robert didn't need impressing, but a pilgrimage of my own would show my new-found resolve. I discussed the nature of this pilgrimage with Robert and we decided that I should retrace the few steps made on that fateful morning, but this time would carry on to York seeking alms for the poor. And to show my resolve the trip would be achieved bare-foot. No matter that it was winter and the ground frozen.

Whilst my birthing into Robert's little community had not been without its challenges, I now began to find a new confidence. Robert and I were true companions. We increasingly found ourselves second guessing each other's response to a situation of need, and together we lived out the golden rule at the heart of Robert's calling – love of God and of neighbour. Living by this different rule was of course made easier by our relative isolation. But then the constant flow of visitors, and our dealings with traders and townsfolk in Knaresborough, meant we were far from being cut-off.

Several harvests passed. The resident group, our community of brothers, saw some comings and goings. And the distances that people were prepared to travel to visit Robert continued to surprise me. They were always warmly welcomed both at the cave and through the hospitality of the townsfolk in Knaresborough. However, Robert's real passion was for the locals. He was no respecter of persons. Position, influence or power never got in the way of spotting the real needs of those who came. And despite my early scepticism his generosity didn't mean he was to be taken advantage of. I remember the time when someone from the town acted as if crippled to secure alms, and the look on his face when Robert decreed that he might be fixed in the infirmity he was acting out. I was glad on that occasion that Robert also had a merciful soul and sent the man packing without following through.

And even where there was no intent to deceive, Robert could see through to people's real needs. Life's difficulties happened sure enough, and the world could be a cruel place. But so often people asked for a balm for their physical symptoms when it was a sickness of their spirit that needed to be addressed.

Robert continued to mentor me, encouraging the right attitude toward things of the world, to possessions, passions and people. 'Don't worry', was a favourite refrain, taken straight from the lips of Jesus. 'Look at nature around you', he would say, 'so beautiful, and so wonderfully provided for. And our Lord loves you far more than these'. The logic was clear to Robert and went to the heart of the work of our community. We were subject to a different overlord, which meant living by a different rule. 'Look out for God's kingdom first', he'd remind me, 'and God will make sure you're provided for!'

It was with these experiences seared into my life and soul that I stood that morning witnessing the visit of King John. The meeting between this unexpected pilgrim and Robert would surely show me what can happen when two kingdoms compete for primacy. For John, the challenges of holding on to his kingdom were etched on his face as he stood opposing Robert. Even this apparent act of penance in offering alms to Robert could be interpreted as a bit of a rescue mission for his kingdom, and possibly his soul. He was calling in all possible allies and, having been excommunicated and then reconciled to the Church in recent years, here was an opportunity to make a few things good. At least, that is what he had been told by his own steward, Sir Brian L'Isle.

I looked at the royal visiting party and considered their finery. In my head, I multiplied it all a hundred times, a thousand times, and more. Even the most advanced counting table would've struggled to calculate the value of what stood in front of us. I tried to imagine what it would mean to see it all dissolve into silver pennies, and to see these distributed to those in need across the kingdom – not just the meagre and symbolic Maundy distribution John had enacted some five years earlier, but a reversal of the swinging levels of taxation with which this very man had burdened his people over recent years.

I wondered what was going through Robert's mind. Did he feel the same as me? Surely, he would see King John's true motives just as much as he did any other pilgrim? Perhaps he sensed a genuine penance, although personally I doubted that. There was already an air of embarrassment amongst the royal party because Robert had remained in prayer when Sir Brian announced their presence. I knew there was nothing wrong with his hearing, but perhaps his failing eyesight caused a deepening of the unease when he eventually came from his prayers. "Which one is the King?", I heard him say to Sir Brian.

And so, here they now stood, facing each other. Representatives of two rules, two kingdoms, two interlocking spheres of reality. It was Robert who made the first gesture. Holding an ear of corn out in front of him, and speaking in a reverential tone, he said "Is your power such, my lord king, that you can make something like this out of nothing?"

I heard murmurs from the rest of the royal retinue. 'He's mad', some were saying under their breath. Others were clearly impressed with what they assumed was a wise saying but combing their beards with their hands didn't mean that they understood! It was for the King to respond. Perhaps because of the gracious way in which Robert had addressed him, perhaps because he was genuinely challenged, or I fancy because he wanted to get to the point of the visit, he passed over Robert's question and made what seemed like a pre-prepared statement. "Robert", he said, "ask me for anything you need, and I will not delay in granting your request."

'Anything?', I thought, and my previous fantasy came back into mind. It wouldn't have taken long to compile a list, and I wondered if Robert would turn to me at any moment and ask for advice. My mind was racing, and it came as a bit of a shock even to me when Robert responded, "I have all the transitory goods in abundance and I have no need of money." It was true that last year's harvest had been good and the winter not too harsh, which meant that the stores were still adequately stocked, but surely!

Robert continued, "The Christian", and of course King John was back in favour with the Church and so matched that description, "needs to seek nothing except Christ." You could hear a penny drop. It was clear that this personal challenge cut to the quick. I thought to myself how the tables have turned, who was the one in need now? As King John turned to leave I saw a stern look of reproach targeted at Sir Brian, as if to say, 'Fat lot of good this trip turned out to be'.

But I was also left bemused and thought that perhaps a similar comment would be appropriate. And so, when the visiting party was out of earshot I turned to Robert and asked, "But what about the poor? Think of what we could have done with the King's donation...".

Robert didn't answer me immediately, but we retired to the cave together and sat for a while. Clearly a royal visitation didn't happen every day and coming pretty much unannounced always brought its risks. I tried once again to reason things out with Robert, being sympathetic to the situation, and to why he might have responded as he did. But whichever way I did the sums, or the logic, this seemed to have been a missed opportunity. Robert allowed me to talk it through, as if to exhaust the possible explanations. And then, when I'd pretty much run out of ideas, he asked, "And what about the King?"

He paused, and then continued. "King John is a man before God just like you and me. As you know, we are no respecter of rank when all these pilgrims come to our door, and it's the same with God who sees to the heart of every person's need. If we are to be obedient, then even when it is an earthly King standing in front of us our duty to God is the same. We must see that person's need, not our own." He continued, "You know that all things come from God and that we are therefore not dependent on gifts from men. So, if the offer of money, land or any other means by which we seek to serve others comes because the giver is looking to gain something in return, then we know it is not from God, and we do the giver a service in making that clear."

From this new perspective, I reflected again on the royal party that we had entertained that day. As well as Sir Brian, there had been plenty of other high-flying dignitaries – I could tell that from the standards they carried. Perhaps, Robert and I thought, their presence was less innocent than initially thought. It had not been long ago that King John had been escorted in similar fashion to a meadow called Runnymede where a group of barons had got their way and effected one royal stand down. Seeing the King make amends for other misdeeds of his reign through the giving of alms, and to one of the most noteworthy saints of the day, would have been very convenient for these barons as they propped up an ageing monarch.

As these thoughts paced through our minds, and as the possibilities clicked into some sort of order, Robert and I knelt and prayed. It was a prayer for the King. Not for the institution, though it certainly needed it, but for John himself. When we came out of the cave, the sun still high in the sky, Robert turned to me and said "I'll be back in a while. I have a personal message for the King."

It was a dangerous thing to do, not just because of King John's reputation. There was also the entourage, many of whom would have felt equally snubbed by the happenings of the day. But I knew Robert's resolve, and as he went I did what I normally left to him. I returned to the cave and once again knelt to pray, committing myself to stay there until his return.

It was several hours before I heard the other members of our community greeting Robert. During that time, I had alternated between fervent prayer, doubts about whether Robert would ever return, and hunger. But I had remained at my post. When I came out of the cave I saw Robert smiling contentedly.

His first words to me were "You'd better start making plans to bring some more land into production, with plenty of wood for fuel and a reliable food supply for more of the needy – it's a gift from God to extend His kingdom through the hands of his majesty." 'So that's how it works' I thought, although I still have to admit to being a little bemused by the happenings of that day when two kingdoms clashed. Both kingdoms still stood, and there was no bloodshed, but it was clear which of the two had advanced.

# A Band of Brothers

*Nathan, Yvo & Dominic*

### September 1218

Nathan, Yvo and I stood gazing across the scene in front of us. The monks from Fountains Abbey formed something of a guard of honour, whilst the men from the constable's own guard had positioned themselves to check comings and goings. I had made my stand for Robert, but not without great torment and trial at a time that should have been full of peace and reflection. I had been expected to stand with my brothers from Fountains who were intent on returning with Robert's body, but I now sided with Robert's two closest friends at the time of his death.

Robert's wishes had been to lie in rest in the place where his calling had flourished. A testament to the love he felt toward the people of Knaresborough. But it had taken some effort to ensure that these wishes were followed as closely as possible.

I had been chosen by Father John at Fountains to help make preparation for Robert's death, and to arrange for the body to come to lay to rest at the Abbey. Why me? Well, I was the novice monk that set Robert on the path to greater virtue and holy training those 35 years earlier at Newminster. Such was the impression he had made on me that I had remained diligent in prayer concerning his soul from that day to this. In the early years those prayers seemed to disappear into the heavens with no effect. Even when I was transferred to Fountains, knowing that Robert had settled in the area, I still heard nothing.

Until, that is, he found patronage with Helena at Rudfarlington. Now my prayers could take on more substance as news trickled in. The news I got was sporadic, and very unpredictable. One day I'd hear about an established and settled house of prayer; and the next about bandits or confrontations with the nobility. My prayers became more fervent. I prayed that Robert would find his true calling, that he would speak truth to power, that he would receive the earthly as well as the spiritual help that he needed.

Now I had the opportunity to get to know those who had been so close to Robert. My few weeks with Nathan and Yvo convinced me that many of those prayers had been answered, although not always in the ways I might have expected! With all my responsibilities at the Abbey I never got close to finding out the true extent of his impact, but Nathan filled me in on that very quickly. I had met him on one of my early trips in this final episode of Robert's life. He showed me the manuscript he had lovingly crafted. Knowing that there would be no more stories to chronicle he entrusted the work to me for copying, something I ensured was undertaken with the greatest of care and diligence.

But now I was left in a difficult position. My reunion with Robert had been sweet, but it became clear very quickly that there was a strong disagreement between him and Fountains about what should be done when he died. Father John might have anticipated resistance, sending me thinking that I would have some influence over Robert, having been something of a spiritual mentor to him. But any illusions in that direction quickly evaporated.

I was left negotiating and failing to convince my superiors about the extent of Robert's resistance to their ideas, as well as of the bond of friendship that made people like Yvo and Nathan so firm in their support. In the end, I was simply side-lined. Thought of as weak, even disobedient. Father John came to the funeral fully intent on removing the body for burial at Fountains. He had told me many times that Robert's body needed to come to rest in an appropriate place to support future pilgrims, and a place that could keep appropriate records of any miracles that might take place when those pilgrims came. But Robert had spurned such attention in life and would do so in death.

It was only yesterday that John's determination, and my failure to influence the situation, finally became clear. I had finished morning prayers in the silence and tranquility of the idyllic surroundings of the Abbey. But as I sat to break my fast I could hear noises outside. Shovels, carts, bridles clacking and men talking. They did their work as quietly as possible, but with clear intent on getting a job done. This, I realised, was preparation for Robert's burial, here at Fountains.

I had been making regular trips to Robert's community by this stage, and today was to be my last. I was expecting to lodge with Yvo that night before the funeral on the next day. Having witnessed the preparations at the Abbey my progress to Knaresborough that morning was much quicker and more earnest than before. I felt my only option was to warn Yvo, to plead with him that perhaps the best thing to do was to allow Robert's body to be taken after all.

I arrived around noon, tired and gasping for some refreshment, which Yvo quickly provided. 'Why so fraught, brother Dominic', he asked, 'it's not like you to come so quick and early. We need to keep all our strength for today, and tomorrow. Come now, take some rest.' I sat for long enough to compose myself, but my heart was still racing. 'It's Father John', I said. 'It's clear that he intends to seize Robert's body if necessary. I've seen the preparations at the Abbey. We must think about this carefully.'

I was met with stony silence. Could it be that I was being cast as a traitor by both sides? I tried to fill the silence with the reasons why Robert's body being taken to the Abbey might be a good idea. I told Yvo about how it had been for other renowned holy men over the years, and how it had quickened their passage to Sainthood. But precedent never worked for Robert and wouldn't work with Yvo either. I was lost for what to do.

'Dominic', Yvo broke in. 'I understand the difficult position you're in. But we must do everything in our power to resist this. I know what the people of Knaresborough will think, and I know how they can turn. They have the deepest respect for Robert, but they've got the spirit of rebellion in them when pushed, and establishment figures have never sat too well with most of the townsfolk. That's why Robert was so loved. He stood up to this sort of bullying.'

I felt helpless, fearful that such a saintly life would end with a confrontation. Whichever way it went there'd be no happy ending now. I watched as Yvo walked off purposefully in the direction of the town. He didn't say what his plan was. Perhaps it was still forming. I sat motionless for a few minutes, but quickly realised that whatever Yvo could achieve there was still much to do. Staying busy was best, and I realised anyway that the situation was completely out of my hands. Father John and Yvo were each working on plans that were irreconcilable.

As I rose to attend to the local preparations I managed to release a quick prayer – 'please God, work a final miracle for Robert and may he truly rest in peace.'

After the hard work of the day I had not had a chance to find out what Yvo had arranged. That night we slept soundly, and people began arriving early the next day. But not before the constable's men had taken up position. It came as a bit of a shock to me as I rose from morning prayers in Robert's rocky sanctuary to see sentries posted along the path leading to the small chapel that would host the ceremony. They were not threatening and didn't block anybody's way – more a reassurance than a threat. And they were quite polite, even jovial with people as they gathered. It seemed that Yvo had described the potential for civil unrest to the local constable sufficiently well to see that the castle guards were deployed.

In the event, therefore, Robert's funeral and subsequent burial passed off without serious incident. Most of the people there would not have known of the risks, or the preparations that had to be made. When I reflected on it later I suppose there was an inevitability that a life in which two kingdoms were often pitted against each other would reflect a similar drama right to the very end. But Robert was now laid to rest, waiting for the resurrection he hoped for. A resurrection to a world in which there would be no more conflict, no more tears, no more 'left-behinds', and in which the kingdom that Robert dreamt of would be fully realised.

I didn't have many years left to live myself, and until that episode I had thought that there was little more to learn. But meeting Robert again, working with those that he had helped to nurture, and reading the stories of the real lives he touched, I certainly prayed 'thy kingdom come' with much greater understanding from that day on. 'Thy Kingdom come', yes, and 'on earth as in heaven'.